Wicca Candle Spells

Simple Wiccan candle spells, rituals, and witchcraft that work fast!

Table Of Contents

Introduction	1
Chapter 1: What You Need To Know About Wicca	2
Chapter 2: Rituals And The Necessary Tools	5
Chapter 3: Simple Candle Spells	11
Chapter 4: The Eight Pagan Sabbaths	17
Chapter 5: Common Misconceptions About Wicca	20
Conclusion	24

Introduction

I want to thank you and congratulate you for downloading the book, "Wicca Candle Spells".

This book contains helpful information about Wiccan candle spells, and how you can do them!

You will also learn about Wiccan history, culture, and beliefs. There are many misconceptions and myths about Wicca, and these will be dispelled and explained throughout the course of this book.

As you will discover, there are different Wiccan spells for many different goals and purposes. Many of the Wiccan spells involve the use of candles.

You will learn what colored candles to use for different spells and rituals, and also how to create your own candle spells and incantations.

This book will explain to you tips and techniques that will allow you to begin successfully using Wiccan candle spells for increased success, improved relationships, and more!

So read on, and let's begin!

Thanks again for downloading this book, I hope you enjoy it!

Chapter 1:
What You Need To Know About Wicca

For many people, simply hearing of the word "Wicca" brings to mind images of witchcraft and dark magic. However, this is most certainly not the case when it comes to this particular belief system. As a matter of fact, the general public's idea of it has been clouded by years and years of lies as well as misinformation. Whether it be something that they've been taught to believe or what they have absorbed through the media's representation of Wicca, the idea of it being cloaked in darkness is certainly false.

Wicca, for those who take the time to really learn more about it, is actually a very balanced way of living. Harmony and peace as well as promoting oneness with all that exists and with the divine is just some of the things that it teaches. Wicca or witchcraft, as it is known more commonly, was known in ancient history as "The Craft of The Wise". This is because many who followed this belief were more in tune when it came to the different forces of nature and were knowledgeable about different natural medicines that could be harvested from the land. Many of them served as doctors, shamans, leaders and healers of their time.

These men and women understood the idea that mankind is not superior to nature, the creatures of the earth and the land itself. Instead, they knew that we were just a part of something bigger and everything combined much like moving parts to piece together the whole.

However, things changed when myths about the belief began to spread. The medieval church began to try and convert those who followed nature based religions into conforming to the church's way of thinking. They turned the idea of witchcraft into something diabolical, something evil that people must stay away from. The nature deities became devils and demons. Soon enough, witch hunters entered the picture as the church tried to stamp out what was left of the belief itself. Many died for their belief but many hid and adopted a new name for it in order to escape persecution. This is why it is also known as Wicca today.

Wicca's Core Beliefs:

Wicca is a spiritual system that puts emphasis on the free will and free thought of every individual. It encourages people to learn more about the earth and nature as well as deepen their understanding of it. In doing so, they hope that it would re-affirm in people the belief that divinity is in every living thing that exists on this earth. Beyond that, it teaches people to become responsible. For many people, it is much easier to blame someone else or an external force when it comes to any of the mistakes, shortcomings and weaknesses that they have. Wicca teaches us that these things are our responsibility and not anyone else's, that everything that happens to us are the consequences of our own choices.

The thing that most people recognize, however, would be Wicca's association with spells and mysticism. Yes, it is a nature based belief and many practitioners do believe in nature deities. They also acknowledge the different nature cycles, the lunar phases which are known to affect the earth (proven scientifically!) and the seasons where they celebrate and worship the divine. It is living with the intent of achieving a balance with all things and living in harmony with nature itself - something that many modern men and women tend to disregard.

Wiccans also believe that the spirit of the one, the goddess and the god, is inside all things. It exists everywhere - in the flowers, the sea, the rain, in all the creatures of the earth and in us as well. This is why they also value life itself and understand the simple fact that we must treat everything on earth as a part of the divine. They honor and respect life in all of its forms, both seen and unseen.

This is the aspect of Wicca that people rarely ever get to see represented in the media and in the public eye. However, this is the reality of things. It is all about becoming one with nature, the elements; and living according to its rhythm, getting in touch with the inner self in order to connect with the universal energy. It is a belief that fosters reverence for the environment and all life upon this earth, something that you'll find recurring in many different religions throughout the world.

Chapter 2:
Rituals And The Necessary Tools

Yes, there are such things as spells and rituals that can be performed to achieve certain goals, whether it be personal or for someone else. These spells often involve boosting harmony and love, wisdom, beauty, and promote healing. Contrary to what most people would imagine, rarely do these spells get used for something dark and unsavory. Potions are also made as tonics, to help a person relieve themselves of an awful cold or a headache. All of which are natural and make use of what nature has to offer while keeping in mind that everything taken must also be given back.

For rituals, there are certain tools that are used in order to properly direct the energy according to the need. These aren't mandatory, but they can help in strengthening a spell or ritual. Here are a few of the most commonly used ones:

– The Athame

The name might be a little misleading because while it is a knife, it is not something that is used for cutting things up. Instead, it is used as a means of directing energy during the ritual itself. The Athame is typically dull and double-edged with a black or dark-colored handle. You can have your Athame engraved with different magical symbols but this is not necessary.

For rituals, the sword serves the same purpose as this knife. They are both associated with the element of fire and because of their phallic resemblance, they are also often used to represent the God.

- The Besom

Also known as the witch's broomstick, this is one of the most enduring symbols of witchcraft as a whole. However, contrary to popular belief, they were never used for flying. The idea of a witch in flight was simply the layman's attempt to describe their observation of astral projection.

The real purpose of the besom was to symbolically clean the space where the ritual is being performed. It gets rid of any negative energy and is usually done before and after the ritual itself.

- The Cauldron

This is the traditional vessel for both brewing and cooking in Wicca but it also symbolizes a few other things. Transformation, femininity and fertility, it is often associated with the element of water as well as the Goddess. During rituals, the cauldron is often the focal point because of the fact that it is multipurpose. Traditional cauldrons are typically made of cast iron and come with three peg legs to hold them up.

- The Chalice

This serves a similar purpose as the cauldron but in a much smaller capacity. It is also often used for holding the salt water to cleanse different objects, for mixing potions and to hold the ritual wine and various other liquids that are needed. Much like the cauldron, it is also a symbol of the Goddess and is also associated with the element of water as well as fertility.

- The Censer

This is the ceremonial incense burner and holds your incense during any ritual. If you don't have the traditional censer, you can also use an alternative in the form of an old cup or bowl. The act of burning the incense as well as breathing in some of it is often done to promote an altered state of consciousness or to cleanse the area. The censer is typically placed before the images of the deity right on your altar.

Simple Wiccan New Year Ritual:

If you want to give simple rituals a try, this one would be a good one to start with. Samhain is what's known as the Wiccan New Year so do perform this particular ritual in the nights (or days!) leading up to it.

- Tools:

Pen and paper, a black candle, some incense, chalice, water, a small jar and a quartz crystal of any size.

- Process:

Find a place where it's quiet and comfortable. This is where you'll create a holy space to perform your ritual in. If you have one, somewhere near your altar would be the best space for this purpose. Once you've found your spot, calm both your mind and soul. Focus on your breathing and when you feel relaxed, you can begin.

Take your piece of paper and write your intents for the coming New Year on it. Are you looking for more happiness? Financial stability or a better job? Peace of mind or a new adventure to sink your teeth into? Write generally and make it brief for the universe will definitely bring what is best for you so there's no real need to focus on the specifics. A good sign that things are going well would be a fuzzy, warm feeling that happens while you're writing your intents down.

Now, the ritual really begins. First, you must engage all of the elements one by one. We begin with air.

Air: Light your incense (preferably sage for cleansing) then say these words:

"God and Goddess, Mother and Father

I give thanks for all that I have

With air I cleanse the past to prepare for a prosperous new year

For the highest good, so be it"

Once done, allow the incense smoke to fill up the air around you whilst you let all the negativity within you leave your energy field. You can visualize a bright light surrounding you as well; allow it to grow brighter and brighter, changing colors with every breath that you take.

Don't forget to whisper a thank you after each prayer you make.

Fire: Light your black candle (preferably made from something organic like beeswax). This candle will actually absorb all the negativity and get rid of it. It also helps you connect with both resilience and self-control while offering you strength. Black is also the color of Samhain. As you proceed in lighting up the candle, contemplate on the experiences you have been through in the past year and focus on expelling any of the heaviness that resulted from it. Allow it to disintegrate in the fire and visualize the same fire providing you with the spark and energy you need to move on.

"God and Goddess, Mother and Father

I give thanks for all that I have

With fire I ignite the future

To prepare for a prosperous new year

For the highest good, so be it"

Leave your candle burning until you have finished the entire ritual.

Water: Take your chalice and fill it with the water. Gently cup your hands around it, allowing your energy to become one with the water it contains. You can visualize it moving from you and into the chalice. Doing so should help you focus better. As you do this, allow your heart to be filled with gratitude for the water and all of its life-giving, and purifying properties. Raise your chalice and repeat these words:

"God and Goddess, Mother and Father

I give thanks for all that I have

With water I vitalize the future

To prepare for a prosperous new year

For the highest good, so be it"

Drink the water from the chalice and pay attention to how it feels inside your body. Visualize it reviving, cleansing and energizing your entire being as you do so.

Earth: Take your piece of paper, the one you wrote on earlier, and wrap it around your quartz. This stone will assist you when it comes to manifesting your wishes. Clasp your hands around it and say:

"God and Goddess, Mother and Father

I give thanks for all that I have

With earth I manifest my wishes

To welcome a prosperous new year

For the highest good, so be it"

Now, take your jar and place the stone with the paper in it. Keep it some place safe, where it won't be disturbed. Thank the elements for their presence as well as assistance in the ritual. Send them on their way by patting your floor three times. Try to spend some quiet time by yourself after performing this ritual and visualize the wishes you had as actual manifestations. Let the joy from this come over you and relish the calm satisfaction that it brings. Keep this feeling within you as you finish the ritual and move forward, into the New Year.

Chapter 3:
Simple Candle Spells

Candle rituals and spells have been used for centuries in the Wiccan tradition. When you light the candles, you will need to recite a simple spell or your intentions while visualizing its manifestation in reality. It is a combination of both desire and need. These spells are quite easy to do and only really require focus and your trust in a higher power to provide you with what is needed.

Now, as for the candles, every color has a corresponding meaning. Below is a chart to help you choose the right one for your needs:

- White: Truth and purity
- Red: Love, sex, strength and health
- Green: Fertility, luck, money
- Black: Evil, discord, negativity
- Brown: Hesitation, uncertainty, neutrality
- Pink: Honor, morality, love
- Purple: Ambition, power, progress
- Orange: Stimulation, attraction
- Greenish Yellow: Discord, anger, jealousy
- Gray: Stalemate, neutrality, negativity
- Light Blue: Health, patience, tranquility

- Dark Blue: Changeability, depression

The difficulty of performing these spells varies and often depends on how much time you're actually willing to put into the ritual itself. You can do something simple like lighting the candle and chanting your intentions repeatedly. It can also be something that lasts for days, wherein you reposition the candle each day and reciting a more profound spell for your intentions.

To get started with it, you will need the right color candle for your needs. After this, you will have to anoint this candle with some oil. Olive oil would work well. Rub the candle from the middle, going outwards to the ends of it. As you're performing this, visualize your desired goal. Once done, find a quiet spot where you can meditate on your wishes while lighting the candle. There's no real need to make your spell rhyme, you can make it as simple or as complicated as you want. Keep in mind that this is all about the power of positive thinking and visualizing the manifestation of your wishes. When you do this, you are sending that energy vibration into the universe.

To help you practice, below are some easy to do candle spells that you can try.

Healing Candle Spell

You'll need:

A tool to inscribe on your candles and three blue candles.

How to:

- Arrange your candles in a triangle and make sure there's enough space between them.

- Inscribe the person you want to be healed upon the candles.

- Light them up and concentrate your energy of health, peace and positive energy. At this point, you can also start reciting your intentions. Repeat it three times.

- Meditate while the candles slowly burn away. Imagine the person as being happy, healthy and whole.

Love Candle Spell

You'll need:

A sampler bottle of a scent that you really love, a tool for inscribing and one pink candle.

How to:

- Begin by carving a heart on your candle. Light it after and place it by the window where it might receive some moonlight.

- Put your favorite scent by the candle and recite:

"Venus, send me the love that I need.

Through this scent, may he or she be attracted."

- Let your candle burn out after and carry the scent with you. Spray it on whenever you're out meeting people. If you repeat the incantation while you spritz it on, it will help increase its potency.

Protection Candle Spell

You'll need:

One red candle and your choice of protective herb.

How to:

- Begin by encircling your candle with your protection herb.

- Light the wick after and gaze into the fire, make sure that you're not too close to it. Focus your energy and once you feel ready, recite your intentions.

- Let the candle burn out while you meditate on your incantation.

Cleansing/Purification Candle Spell

You'll need:

One white candle and a cup of salt.

How to:

- Place your candle in the middle of the room you wish to cleanse.

- Sprinkle your salt, clockwise, around your candle.

- Light it and focus your energy before reciting your intentions.

Clearing Out Spirits Candle Spell

You'll need:

One white candle and some sea salt.

How to:

- Begin by putting all of the salt in a small bag that you can carry around. You'll be sprinkling this in every room.

- Hold the candle with your right hand then light it. Take some of the salt with your left.

- Start walking backwards through your house and go into every room. Sprinkle just a bit of salt in the corners of each room while you repeat your intention. "Ghosts and spirits, leave this place and be gone. Never return."

- Once you reach the northernmost part of your house, snuff out your candle.

Prosperity Candle Spell

You'll need:

One green candle, one white candle and any oil of your choice.

How to:

- The green candle represents money and the white one would represent you. Start by anointing the candles with the oil. As you do this, focus on your intent to prosper financially.

- Once done, set your candles on an altar or any table available. Make sure that they are nine inches apart. After you're done, recite your intentions out loud.

- Repeat this process for nine days, at the same time everyday. Whenever you do, make sure that you also move the white candle an inch closer to the green one. By the time your spell is finished, they should be touching each other.

Assistance With Studying Candle Spell

You'll need:

A yellow candle, a carving tool, pen and paper, and a flame proof dish.

How to:

- Gather all of the things that you need for studying or perform this spell in your study area. Create a circle and carve a symbol, a rune for wisdom and insight would do, onto the candle.

- Light it up and meditate on what you want. Find your focus and direct it towards the candle you're holding.

- Recite your wishes out loud. After this, draw the rune for disordered thoughts on the piece of paper and set it alight. Place it on the fire proof dish and watch as it turns to ash.

- Don't forget to visualize all of your distractions going up in flames too. Keep your candle lit while you study and if it goes out, simply light it again or get a new one (repeat the spell) if it burns down.

Chapter 4:
The Eight Pagan Sabbaths

The Sabbath comprises the foundation for many of Paganism's modern traditions. There is a rich history behind each one of them which, if you're just starting out with Wicca, is something that's worth learning about.

- Samhain: Every year on October 31st (or May 1st if you live in the Southern Hemisphere) this Sabbath celebrates the cycle of death and rebirth. It is quite fitting as this is also the time of year when the earth has gone dormant. This is the time for reconnecting with the ancestors as well as honor those who have passed. It has been said that during this time, the veil that divides the world of the living and the spirits becomes thin thus making it the best time to contact the dead.

- Winter Solstice: For many people, regardless of their religious beliefs, this is the time for gathering with the family and friends. For pagans, it is usually celebrated as Yule but there are many different ways to celebrate it. The idea is to welcome warmth and light into your house, filling it with love and ridding it of any negative energy. This season is filled with magic and focuses on renewal as well as rebirth.

- Imbolc: By the time February comes around, most people are tired of the snow and the cold. Imbolc is the Sabbath that reminds us that soon, springtime will come. During this time, the earth gets a little warmer and the sun, just a bit brighter. Much like the Winter Solstice, this can be celebrated in a number of different ways. Some people tend to focus on Brighid (Celtic goddess). Others would direct their rituals towards the different seasonal cycles. Imbolc is the time for the feminine aspect of the goddess and all magical energy associated with it. It is also a great time to focus on divination and developing your own magical abilities.

- Spring Equinox: With spring's arrival, the earth awakens and everything comes back to life. Depending on the tradition you follow, this can be celebrated in different ways. Typically, however, rituals are directed towards gratefulness for the fertility of the land as well as the other occurrences that happen along with it; the ground becomes warmer and the different plants slowly unfold themselves to welcome the glowing sun. There are no set rules or boundaries for how it should be celebrated, so just get a feel for your surroundings, you'll know how to welcome the season just by doing that.

- Beltane: Celebrations surrounding this Sabbath are usually directed towards fertility. Often observed on May 1st, the festivities begin the night before in order to "greet" the abundant and fertile earth. Though this particular day has had a long and rather scandalous reputation, it is still one of the most celebrated. Earth opens up to the fertility god and through this union, new life is brought upon the earth. It is also known as the season of fertility and fire, two things which are often reflected in the magic seen in this season.

- Summer Solstice: Gardens are in bloom and summer is at its peak. This Sabbath honors the longest day of the year so in order to celebrate, spend as much time as you can outdoors. You can also perform rituals that celebrate Litha as well as the power of the sun itself.

Pray for prosperity and abundance in your life; whether it be happiness, love, harmony or money. Just make sure that you attract only good energy during this time and bring that home with you after the day is done.

- Lammas: Also known as Lughnasadh, it is representative of the season for reaping what you have sown in the past months. It is also a time for reflection and recognizing that the summer days are slowly dwindling and will soon come to an end. Lugh is the Celtic god that is often celebrated during this season but this is dependent upon your tradition and preferences. Send your gratefulness towards the heavens and the earth for providing you with the food you have on your table.

- Mabon: More commonly known as the autumn equinox, this is the time of year when the fields are slowly becoming empty for the crops have all been reaped and stored for winter. It is a mid-harvest festival during which, one must take some time off from working to honor the changing of the seasons as well as give thanks for the bounty. It is, by tradition, a time of giving thanks for any blessings that you may have received. Celebrate the gifts of the earth and the warmth that you have been given. Recognize the cold that is soon to come and accept all these changes.

Chapter 5:
Common Misconceptions About Wicca

As we've pointed out in a previous chapter, there are countless misconceptions about Wicca. If you're really keen on getting started with this practice, it is important that you know exactly what it is and what it isn't. Shall we get started?

- Wicca or witchcraft is not a cult. There's no such thing as recruiting people to join the ranks or getting them to follow leaders.

- Practitioners do not consort with demons or worship Satan. As a matter of fact, Satan himself is a creation of Christian beliefs. Much like followers of other religions, Wiccans do good things, and help others because it is the right thing and not because they are scared that they will go to hell. This is one of the major differences when it comes to these two beliefs.

- There is no such thing as human or animal sacrifice being performed in rituals. These is simply how the media has portrayed Wicca. In fact, doing such a sacrifice violates one of the basic ideologies behind the belief which is to "harm none."

- Wiccans do not steal other people's energy in order to boost theirs or achieve supernatural powers. The energy is drawn from within, from the land and from the divine.

- Wiccans do not make use of nature's energy or that of the universe's to cast spells in the name of revenge. They also do not maliciously hex people. This goes back to the "harm none" law and it is respected by everyone who practices Wicca.

What you must know is that witches carry with them a firm belief in the Law of Three which basically states that anything you sent out into the universe will be returned to your three fold. This applies whether you're doing bad or good things. With this simple rule in mind, a real witch would very much hesitate in hurting or manipulating another for the sake of their own gain. After all, it comes back at a much larger scale than what they threw out.

Of course, this is not to say that all witches are kind and perfect. They are human too, after all, and there will be those who might end up making mistakes in their judgments. There are those who use their knowledge and abilities to help better the world and spread good everywhere. However, there are also those who do the exact opposite for whatever reason or motivation they have. Do remember that the same flaws and weaknesses that human beings are prone to also apply to witches as well.

Wicca FAQs:

– Who do witches worship?

Within the belief, there is a single power referred to as the One or All. It is comprised of everything that has ever been created or existed. However, this energy does not take rule over the universe. It is, in itself, the entire universe. There are some people who might find it hard to call upon or give praise to a faceless divine presence or energy so it is also often personified into two different aspects: the male and the female. The God and Goddess, as they are also known, have also been given different names such as Isis or Odin and so on.

It all depends upon personal preference and what the person feels right for them.

- If Wicca is not evil, why do you prefer black?

Contrary to superstition, black is not the color of evil. Instead, it is the combination of all the different colors as well as all of the vibration rates that light gives off of the material plane. It is also known that this color is a very good conductor of energy and as such, it helps witches to better absorb energy and boost the power of their own thoughts. Black isn't the preferred color for all witches, however. In fact, some of them prefer doing things in the nude to better connect with the energies that are around them.

- Do all witches share the same belief and practice it the same way?

This would be a tricky question to answer. Firstly, Wicca is a religion that puts great emphasis on individuality. Then, there's also the fact that there are a many different sects within the craft itself. In some sense, it can be said that no two groups would practice things the exact same way but since they all share the same core traditions, there would be certain aspects of it that would be similar. The community of witches, however, tends to be very supportive and would provide anyone new with the information that they need.

- What is a book of shadows?

This particular Wiccan tool is of great interest to many. First off, it does not contain the secret of life but it may contain some secrets which the owner might hold dear. Grimoire, as it is also sometimes referred to, is more of a workbook or a journal. It typically contains rituals, spells, herb lore, poetry, discoveries and so on. While the name itself makes the object seem very ominous and dark, this is very far from the truth.

So there you have it, just a few of the most common misconceptions that people have when it comes to witchcraft and witches as a whole. The more you learn about it, the less dark and scary it becomes. All you really need is an open mind and the willingness to discover more.

Conclusion

Thank you again for downloading this book!

I hope this book was able to help you learn more about Wicca candle spells!

The next step is to put this information to use, and begin using candle spells to improve your life!

Finally, if you enjoyed this book, please take the time to share your thoughts and post a review on Amazon. It'd be greatly appreciated!

Thank you and good luck!

www.ingramcontent.com/pod-product-compliance
Lightning Source LLC
LaVergne TN
LVHW021750060526
838200LV00052B/3563